Nuclear Arms Control: The Strategic Offensive Reductions Treaty

Amy F. Woolf

Specialist in Nuclear Weapons Policy

February 7, 2011

Congressional Research Service

7-5700

www.crs.gov

RL31448

CRS Report for Congress

Prepared for Members and Committees of Congress

Summary

On May 24, 2002, President Bush and Russia's President Putin signed the Strategic Offensive Reductions Treaty (known as the Moscow Treaty). It mandated that the United States and Russia reduce their strategic nuclear weapons to between 1,700 and 2,200 warheads by December 31, 2012. The U.S. Senate gave its advice and consent to ratification on March 6, 2003; the Russian Parliament did the same on May 14, 2003. The treaty entered into force on June 1, 2003, and lapsed on February 5, 2011, when the New START Treaty entered into force.

Russia entered the negotiations seeking a "legally binding document" that would contain limits, definitions, counting rules and elimination rules that resembled those in the START Treaties. Russia also wanted the treaty to contain a statement noting U.S. missile defenses would not undermine the effectiveness of Russia's offensive forces. The United States preferred a less formal process in which the two nations would state their intentions to reduce their nuclear forces, possibly accompanied by a document outlining added monitoring and transparency measures. Furthermore, the United States had no intention of including restrictions on missile defenses in an agreement outlining reductions in strategic offensive nuclear weapons.

Russia convinced the United States to sign a legally binding treaty, but the United States rejected any limits and counting rules that would require the elimination of delivery vehicles and warheads removed from service. It wanted the flexibility to reduce its forces at its own pace, and to restore warheads to deployed forces if conditions warranted. The treaty contains four substantive Articles. The first limited each side to 1,700-2,200 strategic nuclear warheads, but states that the parties can determine the structure of their forces themselves. The second states that START I remained in force; the parties would use that treaty's verification regime to monitor reductions under the Moscow Treaty. The third established a bilateral implementation commission and the fourth sets December 31, 2012, for the treaty's expiration and noted that either party could withdraw on three months notice.

Under the Moscow Treaty, the United States retained most of the delivery vehicles planned for START II, which would have limited each side to 3,500 warheads. But the United States removed additional warheads from deployed forces and left out of its tally warheads that could be deployed on systems in overhaul or assigned to conventional missions. Russia eliminated many of its existing ballistic missiles and submarines, retaining fewer than 150 multiple warhead ICBMs, around 200 single warhead ICBMs, and 10 ballistic missile submarines.

According to official and unofficial reports, both sides have implemented the treaty smoothly. However, they have not held all the planned consultations, as there has been little to discuss. Instead, the two nations began, in 2006, to hold discussions about the 2009 expiration of the 1991 Strategic Arms Reduction Treaty (START), which contains monitoring provisions that aid with verification of the Moscow Treaty.

This report will no longer be updated.

Contents

Tables

Appendixes

Contacts

On May 24, 2002, President Bush and Russia's President Putin signed the Strategic Offensive Reductions Treaty, known as the Moscow Treaty, that would limit strategic offensive nuclear weapons.[1] In it, the two nations stated that they would reduce strategic nuclear weapons[2] to between 1,700 and 2,200 warheads by December 31, 2012. The treaty lapsed, however, on February 5, 2011, when the New START Treaty entered into force and superseded the Moscow Treaty.[3]

Press reports and public statements in 2002 hailed the Moscow Treaty because it seemed to impose sharp reduction from the 6,000 warhead level mandated by the 1991 Strategic Arms Reduction Treaty (START).[4] However, this treaty differed from past arms control treaties in that it did not include any of the detailed definitions, counting rules, elimination procedures, or monitoring and verification provisions that have become common in treaties signed since the late 1980s. Consequently, a simple comparison of warhead levels counted under START and warhead levels permitted by the Moscow Treaty does not provide a complete view of the likely effects of the Moscow Treaty.

This report provides a brief overview of the two nations' objectives when they began discussions on this treaty and a summary of how they resolved these differences when concluding the negotiations. It then describes the key provisions in the treaty and presents illustrative forces that each side might deploy in the next 10 years. It offers a brief assessment of how each nation fared in achieving its objectives when negotiating this agreement and a summary of reaction from U.S. and Russian commentators. It concludes with a brief review of the issues raised during the treaty's ratification debates.

Background

The first signs of a new arms control dialogue between the United States and Russia appeared after President Bush and President Putin met in Genoa, Italy, during the G-8 summit in July 2001. At that time, the Presidents issued a statement saying that the two nations would "shortly begin intensive consultations on the interrelated subjects of offensive and defensive systems."[5] Each nation had sharply divergent views on the substance and goals for these talks. When discussing offensive force reductions, Russia argued that the two sides should seek agreement on a formal treaty that would limit each side to 1,500 nuclear weapons. The Bush Administration wanted to

---

[1] Officially, the treaty is titled "Treaty on Strategic Offensive Reductions" in English and "Agreement on the Reduction of Strategic Offensive Potentials" in Russian. The two sides were unable to agree on a single name. The United States reportedly did not want to include the word "arms" in the title, as the subject of the reductions, because this would imply that, like the Strategic Arms Reduction Treaty (START), the new treaty would require the actual elimination of weapons. But, the Russian language required a noun as the subject of the reductions. Hence, the Russian title refers to the reduction of "potentials." See Michael Wines, "Treaty of What's Its Name," *New York Times*, May 23, 2002.

[2] As is discussed below, the parties did not define this term.

[3] For details on New START, see CRS Report R41219, *The New START Treaty: Central Limits and Key Provisions*, by Amy F. Woolf

[4] The START Treaty, which was fully implemented in late 2001 and expired in December 2009, limited the United States and Russia to 6,000 attributed warheads on their strategic offensive delivery vehicles. However, because START does not include many bomber weapons in its tally, the United States could deploy around 7,100 warheads on its existing nuclear forces structure. Russia, with fewer bomber weapons in its force, had closer to 6,000 weapons.

[5] White House, Office of the Press Secretary. Joint Statement by U.S. President George W. Bush and President of the Russian Federation Vladimir V. Putin on Upcoming Consultations on Strategic Issues. Genoa, Italy, July 22, 2001.

pursue unilateral reductions, with each side setting its own nuclear force size and structure, but it would not offer any details on U.S. plans in this regard until the Department of Defense completed its review of U.S. nuclear posture. This internal review concluded in November, 2001.

During a summit meeting with President Putin in Washington, on November 13, 2001, President Bush announced that the United States would reduce its "operationally deployed" strategic nuclear warheads to a level between 1,700 and 2,200 over the next decade." The President stated that the United States would reduce its forces unilaterally, without signing a formal agreement with Russia. He stated that the two nations did not need "endless hours of arms control discussions" and arms control agreements "to reduce our weaponry in a significant way." He offered to "write it down on a piece of paper," but he indicated that he believed a handshake would be good enough.[6]

President Putin responded by stating that he appreciated the President's decision to reduce U.S. nuclear forces and stated that Russia "will try to respond in kind." He did not offer a target number for the reductions at that time, but he had stated several times in previous months, and repeated in December 2001, that Russia planned to reduce its forces to 1,500 warheads. He did, however, indicate that he would like to use the formal arms control process to reduce U.S. and Russian forces. He emphasized that the two sides should focus on "reaching a reliable and verifiable agreement on further reductions of the U.S. and Russian weapons."[7]

The Negotiations

The two sides began discussions on the form and content of a new agreement in January 2002. Official comments and press reports from January and February 2002 demonstrate that the two sides' opening positions contained significant differences. By the time they concluded the treaty in May, they had resolved most of their differences over form and content. In content, the treaty encodes U.S. proposals. In form, it reflects Russia's desire for a formal, "legally binding" document.

Russian Objectives

Russia entered the negotiations seeking a "legally binding document" that would provide "predictability and transparency" and ensure for the "irreversibility of the reduction of the nuclear forces."[8] In essence, Russia sought a treaty that followed the model used in the Strategic Arms Reduction Treaties (START I and START II), with similar counting rules, elimination rules, and verification procedures, but a lower limit on warheads.

After the Bush Administration's report on the Nuclear Posture Review indicated that the United States planned to hold warheads removed from deployment in storage, Russia also insisted that the new treaty require the elimination of these non-deployed warheads.[9] This would contribute to

---

[6] The White House, Office of the Press Secretary. Press Conference. President Bush and President Putin Discuss New Relationship. November 13, 2001.

[7] Ibid.

[8] Comments of General Yuri Baluyevskiy. U.S. Department of Defense. Under Secretary Feith Joint Media Availability with Russian First Deputy Chief. News Transcript. Washington, January 16, 2002.

[9] Beattie, Alan. "U.S. and Russia Edge Closer to Binding Treaty on N-weapons," *Financial Times*. March 30-31, 2002. (continued...)

the "irreversibility" of the limits; without such a provision, Russia argued the United States might return warheads to deployed systems and exceed the limits in the treaty in a relatively short amount of time. In addition, Russia wanted the treaty to contain a statement noting that the United States would limit its missile defense program so that defenses would not threaten the effectiveness of Russia's offensive forces.[10]

U.S. Objectives

When the negotiations began, the United States did not plan to conclude a formal treaty that would include strict limits on deployed weapons. It wanted to maintain the flexibility to size and structure its nuclear forces in response to its own needs. The United States preferred a less formal process, such as the exchange of letters, in which the two nations would state their intentions to reduce their nuclear forces. They might conclude a joint declaration to provide for added transparency measures so that each side could "understand each other's force structures."[11] Furthermore, the United States had no intention of including restrictions on missile defenses in an agreement outlining reductions in strategic offensive nuclear weapons.[12]

Reaching an Agreement

Form of the Agreement

Press reports indicate that, within the Bush Administration, Pentagon officials argued strongly against incorporating any limits on offensive nuclear weapons in a "legally binding" arms control agreement. They wanted the United States to be able to reduce *or* increase its nuclear forces in response to changes in the international security environment. Secretary of State Powell, on the other hand, supported the conclusion of a "legally binding" agreement because he believed it would help President Putin's standing with domestic critics who opposed his policies towards the United States.[13]

The United States apparently began to move towards Russia's position in early February 2002. In a hearing before the Senate Foreign Relations Committee, Secretary of State Powell said that the framework "will be something that is legally binding, and we are examining different ways in which this can happen."[14] According to Secretary Powell, the Administration could complete the agreement as an executive agreement, whose approval would be subject to a majority vote of both houses of Congress, or a formal treaty, which would require the consent of two-thirds of the members of the Senate. Some in the Pentagon, however, continued to oppose the conclusion of a

---

(...continued)

See, also Purdhum, Todd S. "Russia Calls for Binding Pact to Reduce Nuclear Arsenals," *New York Times*, January 31, 2002; and Slevin, Peter. "U.S. Russia Divided on Nuclear Arms Cuts," *Washington Post*. April 28, 2002. p. 25.

[10] Russia Foreign Minister Urges U.S. to Discuss 'Real' Arms Cuts," *Dow Jones International News Service*. February 27, 2002.

[11] U.S. Department of Defense. Special Briefing on the Russian Visit. News Transcript. Washington, January 16, 2002.

[12] Kralev, Nicholas. "U.S. Russia Reach Stalemate on Arms," *Washington Times*. February 20, 2002. p. 9.

[13] Landay, Jonathan. "Rumsfeld Reportedly Resists Firm Limits on Nuclear Arms," *San Jose Mercury News*. April 27, 2002.

[14] Purdum, Todd S. "Powell Says U.S. Plans to Work out Binding Arms Pact," *New York Times*. February 6, 2002. p. 1.

treaty limiting strategic offensive nuclear weapons. They preferred to limit any "legally binding" provisions to procedures for verifying the number of deployed warheads.[15] In testimony before the Senate Armed Services Committee in February, Undersecretary of Defense Douglas Feith said "we see no reason to try to dictate the size and composition of Russia's strategic forces by legal means" and "we do not believe it is prudent to set in stone the level and type of U.S. nuclear capabilities."[16]

President Bush appeared to endorse Secretary Powell's approach in March. He agreed to sign a legally binding agreement, noting that "there needs to be a document that outlives both of us." He also stated that the exact form of this "legally binding" document had not been decided. But he also endorsed the Pentagon's emphasis on verification. He indicated that the agreement should focus on verification, calling it "the most important thing."[17]

In mid-March, Senators Joseph Biden and Jesse Helms sent a letter to the White House reportedly "demanding" that the Administration submit the eventual agreement to the Senate as a treaty. They noted that "significant obligations by the United States regarding deployed U.S. strategic nuclear warheads" would "constitute a treaty subject to the advice and consent of the Senate."[18] This letter demonstrated that both parties in the Senate agreed on the need to defend the Senate's prerogatives and supported its right to advise and consent on treaties. The White House did not accept the Senate's position immediately. However, when the President announced, on May 13, that the United States and Russia had reached an agreement, he stated that it would be a treaty.[19] One Administration official noted that the Senators' position had contributed to the change in the U.S. position in discussions with Russia.[20]

Content of the Agreement

The United States and Russia disagreed about several key issues that would be addressed by the proposed arms control agreement. These included the definitions and counting rules that the two sides would use to calculate how many warheads should count under the treaty's limits; the disposition of warheads removed from deployed systems; transparency and verification provisions; and potential restraints on missile defenses.

Limits and Counting Rules

The U.S. and Russian differences over how to count the weapons limited by the Moscow Treaty persisted throughout the negotiations. Russia proposed that the treaty use counting rules similar to those in START to calculate the number of warheads on deployed weapons.[21] Under START, the

---

[15] Landay, Jonathan. "Rumsfeld Reportedly Resists Firm Limits on Nuclear Arms," *San Jose Mercury News*. April 27, 2002.

[16] Bleek, Phillip C. "U.S., Russia Agree to Codify Nuclear Reductions," *Arms Control Today*. March 2002.

[17] Pincus, Walter. "Bush Backs an Accord on Nuclear Arms Cuts," *Washington Post*. March 14, 2002. p. 19.

[18] Shanker, Thom. "Senators Insist on Role in Nuclear Arms Deals," *New York Times*. March 17, 2002. p. 16.

[19] White House, Office of the Press Secretary. President Announces Nuclear Arms Treaty with Russia. May 13, 2002.

[20] Purdum, Todd S. "Powell Says U.S. Plans to Work out Binding Arms Pact," *New York Times*. February 6, 2002. p. 1.

[21] The number of warheads assigned to ICBMs and SLBMs usually equals the number carried by each type of system. Bombers that were not equipped with cruise missiles would count as one warhead, regardless of the number of weapons they carried. U.S. bombers equipped with cruise missiles would count as 10 warheads, but could carry up to 20 cruise missiles. Russian bombers equipped with cruise missiles would count as 8 warheads but could carry up to 16 (continued...)

parties assign a number of warheads to each type of deployed delivery vehicle (ICBMs, SLBMs, and heavy bombers.) They then "count" the number of deployed delivery vehicles and multiply by the "attributed" number of warheads to calculate the total number of warheads that would count under the treaty limits. To remove weapons from accountability, the parties could either reduce the deployed number of warheads on missiles, and change the "attributed" number of warheads (a process known as downloading) or destroy the delivery vehicles according to complex procedures outlined in the treaty.[22] However, according to some reports, Russia wanted the Moscow Treaty to count the maximum number of warheads that could be carried by a delivery vehicle, without permitting "downloading" to reduce that number.[23] The parties would have to destroy delivery vehicles to reduce the number of deployed warheads.

The United States did not plan to use the START counting rules and elimination rules to calculate the number of "operationally deployed" warheads. Under the U.S. formula, delivery vehicles that were not deployed with nuclear warheads—either because they were in overhaul or assigned to non-nuclear missions—would not count against the limits. Warheads that had been removed from deployed systems also would not count under the limits. In addition, the parties would not have to eliminate or destroy delivery vehicles or stored warheads to reduce the number of warheads that counted under the agreement.[24]

The United States preferred this approach to the START counting rules because it wanted to maintain the ability to reverse the reductions if conditions warranted. Administration officials also noted that the United States should not have to bear the costs of eliminating launchers and delivery vehicles according to START elimination rules.[25] For example, the Navy had converted 4 Trident submarines, which could carry nearly 800 strategic warheads, to carry conventional weapons; it did not want to remove the ballistic missile launch tubes from the submarines. Similarly, the Air Force assigned many of its heavy bombers to conventional units, rather than nuclear units, on a day-to-day basis. But it did not want to eliminate the aircrafts' ability to deliver nuclear weapons because this would be costly and it could limit aircrafts' conventional capabilities. In addition, the United States plans to have two ballistic missile submarines in overhaul at any one time. The Bush Administration did not count the warheads that could be deployed on these vessels under the treaty's limits. If all weapons that could be carried on these systems counted against the U.S. limits, the United States would retain nearly 4,000 warheads. Hence, the United States could not use the START counting rules to calculate warheads, retain the force structure identified in the Nuclear Posture Review, and reduce its forces to 1,700-2,200 warheads.

Russia apparently realized that, if it was going to complete an agreement imposing any limits on U.S. nuclear weapons, it would have to accept the U.S. refusal to include START counting rules

---

(...continued)

cruise missiles.

[22] According to START, to eliminate ICBMs warheads, the parties had to blow up or excavate the silo that had held the ICBM, to eliminate SLBM warheads, the parties had to remove the launch tubes from ballistic missile submarines, and to eliminate bombers, the parties had cut off the wings and tails, or convert the bombers so that they could no longer carry nuclear weapons.

[23] Gottemoeller, Rose. *The New U.S.-Russian Nuclear Agreement.* Carnegie Endowment for International Peace. Non-Proliferation Project Issue Brief. Vol. V. No. 9. May 13, 2002.

[24] Purdum, Todd S. "Powell Says U.S. Plans to Work out Binding Arms Pact," *New York Times.* February 6, 2002. p. 1.

[25] Slevin, Peter. "U.S. Russia Divided on Nuclear Arms Cuts," *Washington Post.* April 28, 2002. p. 25.

and elimination procedures in the treaty. Russia's acceptance of the U.S. position, which apparently occurred in early May, cleared the way for the treaty's completion.

Non-Deployed Warheads

Russia initially insisted that the Moscow Treaty require the elimination of both delivery vehicles and warheads removed from service. It argued that the treaty must provide for "radical, real, and irreversible" cuts in strategic offensive weapons.[26] The United States, on the other hand, pointed out that previous arms control agreements, such as the START I and START II treaties, had not required the elimination of warheads removed from deployment. Both sides could keep the warheads for testing, spare parts, and possible redeployment.

In mid-March, Russia appeared to acknowledge this point and soften its objection to the U.S. position.[27] Russia's Defense Minister Sergei Ivanov said that "for some period of time, those warheads could be stored or shelved," even though they would eventually have to be eliminated.[28] At the same time, though, Russia sought to address the problem of the "reload capability" through the treaty's counting rules. As was noted above, Russia wanted the treaty to count delivery vehicles as the maximum number of warheads they could carry and to require the elimination of delivery vehicles before their warheads could be removed from the treaty totals. These rules would have eliminated concerns about stored warheads; without the extra delivery vehicles, warheads could not return to the force. But, as was noted above, the Bush Administration rejected this position. It wanted to maintain the ability to redeploy warheads on short notice.[29] By the end of April it was clear that the United States would insist on retaining its delivery vehicles and maintaining an unspecified number of warheads in storage.[30]

In comments published after the treaty was signed, General Yuriy Baluyevskiy, the First Deputy Chief of the Russian General Staff, indicated that he believed the question of warhead storage had not yet been resolved. He stated that the treaty establishes a special bilateral commission on implementation and that the two sides could use this commission to discuss what to do with the warheads removed from deployment.[31] The United States did not endorse this view, and these discussions never occurred.

Verification

The United States recognized that, under its proposed limits, the absence of counting rules and elimination provisions would make it difficult for each side to monitor the number of deployed warheads on the other side.[32] As was noted above, under START, the parties counted the number

---

[26] Purdhum, Todd S. "Russia Calls for Binding Pact to Reduce Nuclear Arsenals," *New York Times*, January 31, 2002.

[27] Bleek, Phillip C. "U.S. and Russia at Odds over Strategic Reductions Treaty," *Arms Control Today*. May 2002.

[28] Pincus, Walter. "Bush Backs an Accord on Nuclear Arms Cuts," *Washington Post*. March 14, 2002. p. 19.

[29] Slevin, Peter. "U.S. Russia Divided on Nuclear Arms Cuts," *Washington Post*. April 28, 2002. p. 25.

[30] LaFraniere, Sharon. "U.S. Russia Report Progress in Nuclear Arms Talks," *Washington Post*, April 30, 2002. p. 14. See also, "U.S. Will Not Destroy Nuclear Warheads, Crouch Says," *Aerospace Daily*. May 2, 2002.

[31] Safronov, Ivan. "Russian General Staff's Baluyevskiy Lauds Strategic Offensive Reductions Treaty," *Moscow Kommersant*, May 27, 2002. Translated in FBIS CEP20020527000221.

[32] Press reports indicate that the U.S. intelligence community told the Administration that Russia could be able to deploy a few hundred warheads, above the 2,200 limit, without detection. See Jonathan S. Landay. "U.S. Unable to Confirm Russia's Compliance with Weapons Treaty," *Knight Ridder Newspapers*. December 20, 2004.

of deployed delivery vehicles and multiplied that number by the agreed "counting rule" for each type of system. They do not count the actual number of warheads in place on the delivery vehicles. The START Treaty permitted on-site inspections that allowed the parties to view reentry vehicles, but these inspections were designed to confirm that the number of warheads *did not exceed* the number allowed for that type of delivery vehicle. They might not be able to identify the actual number of warheads on a missile if it were less than the number in the data base.[33]

During the negotiations, the United States suggested that the two nations include new transparency measures in the agreement. These could include "more detailed exchanges of information, visits to particular sites, additional kinds of inspections, and additional kinds of activities at sites" to enhance confidence and help verify reductions of "operationally deployed systems."[34] For example, the parties could use a reentry vehicle inspection system similar to the one in START, where they declare a number of warheads carried by each type of missile and follow it with inspections that confirm that the actual number does not exceed the declared number. Or they could institute new procedures that would allow inspectors to count the actual number of warheads on each missile. They might also permit inspections at storage sites to count weapons held in those locations.[35]

Russia concurred that the new agreement needed transparency measures and a verification regime. Russian officials also agreed that the Moscow Treaty could draw on the verification regime in START I and include "new transparency and confidence measures" to monitor nuclear warheads.[36] However, reports indicate that the two nations were unable to agree on which START measures to employ and which new measures to include in the agreement. Russia apparently wanted a formal system of inspections and data exchanges, while the United States preferred a less elaborate system that called for cooperation, more generally, instead of specifying numbers and types of inspections permitted at specific facilities.[37] Although the two sides were unable to reach agreement on this issue before signing the treaty at the Moscow summit, they did agree to continue discussions after signing the treaty.[38] These discussions, however, did not occur until 2006, when the two sides began to consider a replacement for the START Treaty.

During hearings before the Senate Foreign Relations Committee, Secretary of State Powell indicated that the two sides would have sufficient opportunities to collect needed data and information each others forces, even without a formal monitoring regime. He noted that the growing level of cooperation between the two, particularly through the Nunn-Lugar Cooperative Threat Reduction Program, provided information and assurances about the status of nuclear weapons programs. In addition, the START I Treaty would remain in force through 2009, and

---

[33] For example, the U.S. Navy designed a shield to place over its reentry vehicles during inspections so that inspectors would not see sensitive design information. These shields had a space for each of the 8 permitted warheads on Trident missiles, hence the inspections could confirm that the number of deployed warheads did not exceed the number permitted. But because the inspectors could not see whether all of the spaces actually contained warheads, they could not determine if the missile carried fewer than 8 warheads.

[34] U.S. Department of Defense. Special Briefing on the Russian Visit. News Transcript. Washington, January 16, 2002.

[35] Aldinger, Charles. "U.S., Russia Discuss Nuclear Cuts," *Moscow Times*. January 15, 2002. p. 4.

[36] Bleek, Phillip C. "U.S., Russia Agree to Codify Nuclear Reductions," *Arms Control Today*. March 2002.

[37] Dao, James. "Nuclear Deal Called Closer After Powell Meets Russian," *New York Times*, May 4, 2002.

[38] White House. Office of the Press Secretary. Text of Joint Declaration. May 24, 2002.

information collected under that treaty's verification regime could also contribute to verification of compliance with the new treaty.[39]

Missile Defense

During the negotiations, Russia insisted that the new agreement reflect "the organic interconnection of strategic defensive and offensive weapons."[40] Russia sought assurances that the U.S. missile defense program would not be directed at or undermine Russia's strategic nuclear deterrent.[41] The United States refused to include language limiting ballistic missile defenses in the text of the new agreement. The U.S. refusal to accept Russia's view does not necessarily indicate that the United States planned to deploy missile defenses that could undermine Russia's deterrent. To the contrary, the Clinton and Bush Administrations both insisted that the U.S. missile defense program was not directed at Russia or its strategic deterrent. Both argued that the United States needed defenses to address emerging threats from other nations who were acquiring ballistic missiles. Nonetheless, the Bush Administration indicated that it did not believe that U.S. missile defenses should be subject to any treaty limits.

The United States and Russia resolved this issue by deferring it to a Joint Declaration that outlines areas of cooperation that the two nations would pursue in their new, more cooperative relationship. This document states that "the United States and Russia have agreed to implement a number of steps aimed at strengthening confidence and increasing transparency in the area of missile defense."[42] These steps could include information exchanges on missile defense programs and tests and reciprocal visits to observe tests. They also agreed to explore areas for cooperation in the development of missile defenses, such as the expansion of joint exercises and the possible conduct of joint research and development programs for missile defense technologies. Although this agreement did not impose any limits on U.S. missile defense programs, it could provide Russia with confidence in its understanding of the goals and capabilities of U.S. missile defense programs if the two sides pursued the cooperative programs.

In spite of periodic meetings over the years, tensions increased in the latter years of the Bush Administration as Russia responded with concerns about U.S. plans to deploy missile defense interceptors and a radar in Poland and the Czech Republic.

The Treaty

The text of the Strategic Offensive Reductions Treaty, or Moscow Treaty, appears in **Appendix A** at the end of this report. It contains a preamble that primarily reviews the relationship between the two nations and their existing arms control obligations, four articles that outline the obligations they have assumed under the new treaty and a fifth article that notes that the parties will register

---

[39] The intelligence community reportedly concluded that an extension of START I to 2012 would ease efforts to verify compliance with the Moscow Treaty. See Jonathan S. Landay. "U.S. Unable to Confirm Russia's Compliance with Weapons Treaty," *Knight Ridder Newspapers*. December 20, 2004.

[40] Shatalova, Irina. "Russian Foreign Ministry: Russia wants to cut strategic arms to 1,700-2,200 warheads," *Itar Tass*. April 24, 2002. Translated in FBIS CEP20020424000141.

[41] "Russia Foreign Minister Urges U.S. to Discuss 'Real' Arms Cuts," *Dow Jones International News Service*. February 27, 2002.

[42] White House. Office of the Press Secretary. Text of Joint Declaration. May 24, 2002.

the treaty at the United Nations. The discussion that follows addresses the contents of the four substantive articles in the treaty.

Article I

Article I contains the only limit in the treaty, stating that the United States and Russia will reduce their "strategic nuclear warheads" to between 1,700 and 2,200 warheads by December 31, 2012. The text does not define "strategic nuclear warheads" and, therefore, does not indicate whether the parties will count only those warheads that are "operationally deployed," all warheads that would count under the START counting rules, or some other quantity of nuclear warheads. The text does, however, refer to the statements made by President Bush in November 2001, when he announced the U.S. intention to reduce its "operationally deployed warheads" and President Putin in November and December 2001, when he indicated that Russia would be willing to reduce its strategic forces to 1,500 warheads. This reference indicates that the United States and Russia could each use their own definition when counting their number of strategic nuclear warheads.

The absence of an agreed definition could create ambiguities and confusion about each side's progress in reducing their forces. However, the Article does not impose any interim limits on forces, or set a pace for the reductions, so ambiguities that arise during the ten year period should not give rise to questions about overall compliance with the treaty. In addition, in the absence of interim limits, each side can set its own pace for the reductions, and even stop or reverse them for a period of time, during the 10-year time frame. As long as each side can demonstrate that its forces do not exceed 2,200 strategic nuclear warheads on December 31, 2012, each will meet its obligations under Article I.

Article I also specifies that each party shall "determine for itself the composition and structure of its strategic offensive arms." It does not limit the number of delivery vehicles, or impose sublimits on specific types of weapons systems within the overall total of strategic nuclear warheads. This differed from past arms control agreements, where the United States favored limits that would "restructure" Soviet or Russian strategic forces. The 1991 START I Treaty contained a sublimit on the number of warheads that could be carried on ballistic missiles, a sublimit on the number of warheads that could be carried on mobile ICBMs, and a requirement for the elimination of half of the Soviet Union's 308 heavy ICBMs. The 1993 START II Treaty contained a sublimit on SLBM warheads, and, in an achievement that was hailed as a major breakthrough in U.S-Russian arms control, a ban on all multiple-warhead ICBMs (MIRVed ICBMs).[43]

The Moscow Treaty clearly indicates, however, that this ban, and all other provisions in the START II Treaty, will not be implemented. The preamble and Article II of the treaty refer to the first Strategic Arms Reduction Treaty as START, not START I. Thus, START II, which never entered into force,[44] is evident in its absence. U.S. and Russian officials have both noted the

---

[43] Many analysts argue that MIRVed ICBMs could be destabilizing in a crisis because one or two attacking warheads could destroy up to 10 warheads on the single missile. Hence, a nation might believe it needs to launch first in a crisis, before it lost its forces to a smaller attack. Russia, in particular, deployed a majority of its warheads on these large missiles. Russia also maintained a monopoly in "heavy" ICBMs, the SS-18s, and the United States had long sought limits on or the elimination of these weapons in the arms control process.

[44] The U.S. Senate gave its advice and consent to ratification in 1996 and the Russian Duma approved the treaty in 2000. But the United States never met conditions that Russia had set before the treaty could enter into force.

demise of START II. Assistant Secretary of Defense J.D. Crouch said "I think we have sort of moved beyond START II... setting it aside and have moved beyond it."[45] In comments made shortly after the Moscow Treaty was signed, Russia's General Baluyevskiy noted that the START II Treaty "never operated" and "should be considered dead."[46] One report indicates that the Defense Minister and Foreign Minister informed the Russian Duma in mid-May 2003 that the treaty had lapsed.[47] Russia officially indicated that START II had lapsed after the United States withdrew from the ABM Treaty in late 2002, thus linking its withdrawal from START II to U.S. withdrawal from the ABM Treaty.[48] Regardless, several Russian commentators have noted that, with the new treaty, Russia was no longer obligated to eliminate all of its MIRVed ICBMs.

Article II

Article II states that the START Treaty (meaning START I) remains in force. The treaty does not elaborate on the reason for this observation. However, in the Article-by-Article analysis provided to Congress, the Administration states that the "purpose of this Article is to make clear that the Moscow Treaty and the START Treaty are separate." The Moscow Treaty did not use the same definitions and counting rules as START and the provisions in START remained in force, unchanged by the new provisions in the Moscow Treaty.[49] Nevertheless, in the Joint Declaration signed by Presidents Bush and Putin on May 24, the parties indicated that the provisions of START "will provide the foundation for providing confidence, transparency, and predictability in further strategic offensive reductions." These provisions include data exchanges that describe the numbers and locations of deployed weapons, notifications when deployed weapons are moved to other locations or when they are scheduled to be eliminated, on-site inspections at deployment and elimination facilities, and other cooperative measures that help the parties gain confidence in their estimates of the number of deployed warheads remaining in each others' arsenals.

Article III

Article III establishes a Bilateral Implementation Commission, and states that the parties will meet in this forum at least twice each year. The treaty does not provide any guidelines or procedures for these meetings. In particular, it does not indicate whether these meetings will focus solely on monitoring and verification of the agreed reductions, or whether it will seek to address other issues relevant to the treaty. In its Fact Sheet on the treaty, the White House states simply that the commission will meet to discuss issues related to the treaty. U.S. officials indicated that the commission would work out additional transparency and verification measures, but this never occurred. Further, it seems unlikely that the United States would pursue negotiations on additional limits in the commission. Russia, however, may have preferred a more

---

[45] U.S. Department of Defense. Special Briefing on the Russian Visit. News Transcript. Washington, January 16, 2002.

[46] Safronov, Ivan. "Now There Simply Cannot be any Recoil; Interview the First Deputy Chief of General Staff," *Kommersant.* May 7, 2002. Translated in FBIS CEP20020527000221.

[47] Odnokolenko, Oleg. "Exchange of Strategic Gifts," *Moscow Itogi.* May 21, 2002. Translated in FBIS CEP20020521000407.

[48] Golotyuk, Yuriy. "START is Dead—Long Live SNP," *Vremya Novostey.* May 23, 2002. Translated in FBIS CEP20020523000370.

[49] Letter of Transmittal and Article-by-Article Analysis of the Treaty on Strategic Offensive Reductions. Arms Control Today. July/August 2002. p. 30.

expansive role for the commission. In particular, several Russian officials and analysts noted that the commission could address limits on or the elimination of warheads removed from service.

Article IV

Article IV has three paragraphs. The first states that the treaty shall be ratified in accordance with the constitutional procedures of each Party. This ensures that the treaty will be "legally binding." The second paragraph states that the treaty will remain in force until December 31, 2012, after which it could be extended or replaced by another agreement. U.S. officials have noted that the treaty could lapse if the two sides decided that no further agreement is necessary.[50] In theory, then, the parties might be able to increase their warheads above the 2,200 limit as soon as the treaty expires.

The third paragraph in Article IV states that either party may withdraw from the treaty on three months' notice. This provision differs from the withdrawal clause in previous treaties in two respects. First, other Treaties, such as the ABM Treaty, START I, and START II, required six months notice before a party could withdraw. Second, these Treaties stated that a party could withdraw from the treaty if "extraordinary events related to the subject matter of this Treaty have jeopardized its supreme interests." The new treaty does not have a similar provision. A party could withdraw for any reason, without justifying its actions by citing "extraordinary events [that] have jeopardized its supreme interests."

Reports indicate that during the negotiations, the United States proposed that the treaty include a withdrawal period of only 45 days. It also sought a provision that would have allowed either side to exceed the limits in the treaty for a short period of time, without withdrawing, if "international geostrategic circumstances" warranted.[51] These proposals reflected the U.S. interest in maintaining a maximum amount of flexibility when reducing its forces. But they were not needed in the final draft. Because the treaty does not contain any interim limits or schedule for reductions, either party can exceed the limits in the treaty at any time leading up to December 31, 2012.

Force Structures Under the Treaty of Moscow

The tables in this section display U.S. and Russian force structures in place in July 2009; as reported in the data base exchanged under the START Treaty.[52] They also show forces that would have been consistent with the limits in the START II Treaty and forces that will be consistent with the limits in the Treaty of Moscow. Although the parties will not implement START II, the report includes these potential forces for comparison with the reductions that might have occurred under the new treaty.

---

[50] Bleek, Philipp C. "U.S. and Russia at Odds over Strategic Reductions Agreement," *Arms Control Today.* May 2002.

[51] Bleek, Philipp C. "Bush Endorses Legally Binding Nuclear Arms Deal with Russia," *Arms Control Today.* April 2002.

[52] This is the most recent data available under START I. The treaty expired on December 5, 2009.

U.S. Force Structure

The United States completed its implementation of START in December 2001. In July 2009, U.S. strategic nuclear forces accountable under START included 500 Minuteman III ICBMs, attributed with between one and three warheads each; 50 Peacekeeper ICBMs, attributed with eight warheads each; 18 Trident submarines equipped with 24 ballistic missiles, attributed with six or eight warheads each; 141 B-52 H bombers; 47 B-1 bombers; and 18 B-2 bombers. The B-52 H bombers can be equipped with up to 20 long-range nuclear-armed cruise missiles, but they count as only 10 warheads under START's counting rules.

The United States eliminated 50 Minuteman III ICBMs and the 50 Peacekeeper missiles, but it did not eliminate the silos for these missiles, so they still counted under the START limits. Further, the number of warheads carried by Minuteman III missiles could have remained constant, at between 500 and 600 warheads, as the number of missiles declined.[53] The United States also converted 4 Trident submarines to carry cruise missiles, but, because it did not remove the SLBM launch tubes, these also continued to count under START. The B-1 bombers are no longer equipped to conduct nuclear missions, but each counted as one warhead under START. B-2 bombers can carry up to 16 gravity bombs, but each also counts as only 1 warhead under START. As **Table 1** shows, this force "counts" as 5,916 warheads under the START limit of 6,000 warheads. If all the weapons that could be deployed on B-52 and B-2 bombers were included, this force would count as more than 7,000 warheads.

Table 1. U.S. Strategic Nuclear Forces

	START I		START II		Treaty of Moscow	
	Launchers	Warheads	Launchers	Warheads	Launchers	Warheads
ICBMs	550	1,600	500	500	450	450-500
SLBMs	432	3,264	336	1,680	288	1,056-1,152
Bombers	206	1,052	97	1,276	77	500-850
Total	1,188	5,916	933	3,456	791	2,200

In 1994, as a part of the first nuclear posture review, the United States identified the force structure that it would deploy under the START II Treaty. This force included 500 single-warhead Minuteman III missiles, 14 Trident submarines equipped with 24 5-warhead SLBMs, 76 B-52 bombers, and 21 B-2 bombers. The B-52 bombers would carry 8, 12, or 20 cruise missiles, and count as the number they were equipped to carry. The B-2 bombers would carry and count as 16 gravity bombs. Hence, the United States would eliminate 4 Trident submarines and 50 Peacekeeper missiles and remove warheads from Minuteman and Trident missiles to reduce to the START II limit of 3,500 warheads.[54]

---

[53] For a more detailed discussion on the status of U.S. nuclear forces, see CRS Report RL33640, *U.S. Strategic Nuclear Forces: Background, Developments, and Issues*, by Amy F. Woolf.

[54] The Air Force completed the deactivation of the Peacekeeper Missiles on September 19, 2005.

The Bush Administration initially indicated that it did not plan to eliminate any of the delivery vehicles that the United States would have retained under the START II Treaty. To reduce that force from 3,500 to 2,200, permitted by the Moscow Treaty, it would remove warheads from deployed ICBMs and SLBMs. However, in February 2006, the Administration announced that it planned to eliminate 50 Minuteman ICBMs. Consequently, the Bush Administration planned to deploy 450 Minuteman III missiles, with 1, 2, or 3 warheads on each missile, and 14 Trident submarines with perhaps 3-6 warheads on each missile. However, it would only count the warheads on 12 submarines under the treaty limits because it planned to keep 2 submarines in overhaul at any given time. Further, the Administration announced, in the 2006 QDR, that it planned to reduce the B-52 fleet to 56 bombers.[55] Because many of these bombers would be assigned to conventional units on a day-to-day basis, the Administration would not count the weapons that could be carried on all of these aircraft under the treaty limits. **Table 1**, above, assumes that approximately 500 cruise missiles for the B-52 bombers would count under the Moscow Treaty limits.[56]

Russia's Force Structure

In July 2009, after implementing START, Russian strategic nuclear forces included 104 10-warhead SS-18 ICBMs, 120 6-warhead SS-19 ICBMs, 176 single warhead SS-25 road-mobile ICBMs, 15 road-mobile single warhead SS-27 ICBMs, and 50 single-warhead, silo-based SS-27 ICBMs. Russia also had 14 accountable ballistic missile submarines, equipped with a number of different types of missiles. Russia's bomber fleet consisted of 76 aircraft—13 Blackjack bombers and 63 Bear H bombers. Under START rules, each of these counts as 8 warheads, but they can be equipped to carry up to 16 cruise missiles. This force counted as 3,897 warheads under the START Treaty in July 2009.

Russia never publicly identified a force structure that it would have deployed under START II. However, START II would have required the elimination of all SS-18 ICBMs. Russia could have retained 105 SS-19 ICBMs, but each missile could carry only 1 warhead. It also might have retained between 400 and 700 single warhead ICBMs. This number would depend on Russia's ability to produce new SS-27 ICBMs. It had planned to produce up to 30 of these missiles per year, but, thus far, has succeeded in adding fewer than 10 per year to its deployed forces. Russia's submarine fleet might have consisted of as many as 13 submarines (5 Typhoons and 8 Delta IVs), or, because it has since retired the missiles for the Typhoon submarines, as few as 6 Delta IVs and, possibly, eventually 4-5 new submarines. The bomber fleet could have remained at the current level of 78 aircraft, but each bomber might carry, and count as, 12 warheads.

As **Table 2** shows, Russia could only reach the START II limits of 3,000-3,500 warheads if it deployed over 800 ICBMs, 13 ballistic missile submarines, and 78 aircraft. Most analysts believe

---

[55] The 109th Congress did not authorize the Administration's request for a reduction in the B-52 fleet to 56 bombers. It required that the Administration retain 76 B-52 bombers. However, because the number of bomber weapons counted under the Moscow Treaty is not related to the number of deployed bombers, this report still assumes that the United States will retain, and count around 500 cruise missiles for the B-52 bombers.

[56] In late 2005, the Undersecretary of Defense approved a budgeting decision that called for a reduction in the B-52 bomber force from 94 to 56 aircraft between 2008 and 2011. It is not clear whether this decision will eventually affect the force size as the document noted that Congress "has repeatedly directed the Air Force to maintain" 94 B-52 aircraft. See U.S. Department of Defense. Air Force Transformation Flight Plan. Program Budget Decision 720. December 20, 2005. p. 5. Regardless, this plan will not affect the number of cruise missiles that might be counted under the Moscow Treaty.

that Russia would not have the economic resources to support this force. This problem underlined Russia's interest in concluding a new agreement that would limit each side to only 1,500 warheads.

Table 2. Russian Strategic Nuclear Forces

	START I		START II		Treaty of Moscow	
	Launchers	**Warheads**	**Launchers**	**Warheads**	**Launchers**	**Warheads**
ICBMs	472	2,018	805	805	300	900
SLBMs	288	1,488	228	1,512	96	384
Bombers	79	632	78	936	65	780
Total	839	4,864	1,111	3,253	461	2,064

Most analysts agree that Russia's strategic nuclear forces will continue to decline during the next 10 years, as it retires aging systems and produces only small numbers of new missiles. However, in the absence of the START II ban on MIRVed ICBMs, Russia might deploy its new ICBMs with three or four warheads, instead of one. If Russia produced 30 of these missiles each year, and deployed each with 3 warheads, and if it retained the existing 6 Delta IV submarines and reduced its bomber fleet to 65 aircraft, it could retain a force of 2,064 warheads. This force is displayed on **Table 2**, above. If, on the other hand, it produced 10 missiles per year and equipped each with a single warhead, then Russia's force would include fewer than 500 ICBM warheads, and a total of only 1,624 warheads.

Assessing the Outcome

Russia's Objectives

As was noted above, Russia entered the negotiations in search of a "legally binding" treaty that would make "radical, real, and irreversible" reductions in U.S. and Russian strategic nuclear weapons.[57] It succeeded in achieving the first of these two objectives. Russian officials and other Russian analysts have stated that this outcome represented a major success for Russian diplomacy.[58] Where the United States initially wanted simply to exchange letters or issue a Joint Declaration, Russia convinced it to negotiate and sign a formal arms control treaty. In doing so, these officials argue, Russia can be assured that, as Russia reduces its nuclear forces in response to economic pressures, the United States will also reduce its nuclear forces so that the two retain a rough nuclear parity. Furthermore, the treaty ensured that the U.S. commitment to reduce its forces would continue to exist after the Bush Administration left office.

More important, according to Russian officials, the signing of a treaty indicated that the United States and Russia remained equal partners in the arms control process, even though Russia could

---

[57] Purdhum, Todd S. "Russia Calls for Binding Pact to Reduce Nuclear Arsenals," *New York Times*, January 31, 2002.

[58] Safronov, Ivan. "The Treaty Could Have Been Better But it is Better than Nothing;" Interview with Duma Deputy Andrey Kokoshin. *Kommersant*. May 24, 2002. Translated in FBIS CEP20020524000232. See also, Sergey Rogov. "Capitulation or Move Toward Partnership? Moscow Must Use the 'Window of Opportunity.'" *Nezavisimaya Gazeta*. May 24, 2002. Translated in FBIS CEP20020524000146.

no longer claim to be a military or economic equal of the United States.[59] Many analysts believe that retaining this "seat at the table" was a key objective for President Putin because it demonstrated to his critics at home that Russia will benefit from his new, more accommodating policies towards the United States and the West.

Russia did not succeed in convincing the United States to adopt the START I counting rules or to eliminate excess delivery vehicles or warheads when implementing the treaty. It also did not convince the United States to include in the treaty a provision stating that U.S. missile defenses would not undermine Russia's offensive deterrent. Russian officials recognize that they were unable to win these points in the negotiations, but they seemed to believe that they could still achieve their objectives. As was noted above, General Baluyevskiy argued that the issue of how to limit and eliminate non-deployed warheads could be on the agenda for the treaty's bilateral commission (although discussions on this issue did not occur). Furthermore, even though the treaty does not contain a direct reference to missile defenses, Russian officials have claimed that Russia achieved its objective of linking offenses and defenses by including in the treaty's preamble a reference to the Bush-Putin statement from the Genoa summit, where they agreed to hold "consultations on the *interrelated* subjects of offensive and defensive systems (emphasis added)."[60] And the Joint Declaration, signed at the same time as the Treaty of Moscow, provides Russia its assurances on the scope and intent of U.S. missile defenses by calling for expanded information exchanges and cooperation.

U.S. Objectives

When the United States entered the negotiations, it sought to avoid signing a formal arms control treaty and to maintain unrestricted flexibility in sizing and structuring its nuclear forces. It did not want any limits on its delivery vehicles or its stockpiled warheads and it did not want any limits on U.S. missile defenses. It succeeded in achieving these last objectives, but did not succeed in avoiding a formal arms control treaty. The Bush Administration reportedly acquiesced to Russia's demands for a formal treaty for three reasons. First, the Administration ensured, by standing firm on U.S. negotiating positions, that the treaty would reflect the U.S. objective of maintaining force structure flexibility. The form of the document ultimately became unimportant when it was clear that the substance would not undermine current U.S. plans. Second, key U.S. Senators had pressured the Administration to conclude a treaty.

Third, some in the United States hoped that the U.S. concession on signing a treaty could strengthen President Putin's (and now, President Medvedev's) ability to cooperate with the United States in other areas of security policy. Many in Russia criticized Putin for supporting the United States in its war on terrorism and allowing U.S. troops access to bases on former Soviet territory. By signing the treaty, the Administration, in essence, rewarded Putin for his cooperation and allowed him to answer his critics with his achievement. However, as the years have passed,

---

[59] Safronov, Ivan. "Now There Simply Cannot be any Recoil"; Interview with First Deputy Chief of General Staff. *Kommersant.* May 7, 2002. Translated in FBIS CEP20020527000221. See also, Sergey Rogov. "Capitulation or Move Toward Partnership? Mocow Must Use the 'Window of Opportunity.'" Nezavisimaya Gazeta. May 24, 2002. Translated in FBIS CEP20020524000146.

[60] Russian Federation Foreign Ministry Information and Press Department. On the Main Provisions of the New Russo-U.S. Treaty on the Reduction of Strategic Offensive Potentials. May 22, 2002. Translated in FBIS CEP20020523000243.

strains and disagreements in the U.S.-Russian relationship continued to surface, leading many to question whether progress in arms control can affect the broader U.S-Russian relationship.

Treaty Ratification

As is stated in Article IV, the treaty must be ratified "in accordance with the constitutional procedures" of each nation before it can enter into force. In Russia, a majority of both houses of Parliament, the Duma and the Federation Council, must vote to approve a Federal Law on Ratification. In the United States, two-thirds of the Members in the Senate must vote to approve a Resolution of Ratification. This has been a relatively simple matter, because legislators in both nations praised the treaty and no one voiced opposition to its approval. However, both nations' legislatures have shown a reluctance in recent years to approve arms control agreements without significant debate and, on occasion, significant reservations. In addition, the Russian Duma has often linked its consideration of arms control treaties to its objections on other aspects of U.S. policy.

For example, in 1999, the U.S. Senate failed to offer its advice and consent to ratification of the Comprehensive Test Ban Treaty. It approved the Chemical Weapons Convention in 1997, but included 28 conditions in its Resolution of Ratification. The Clinton Administration never submitted several 1997 agreements related to the 1972 ABM Treaty, in part because it feared the Senate would reject these agreements and attack the continued viability of the ABM Treaty. The Moscow Treaty did not, however, encounter significant opposition in the Senate. Republican Members praised the treaty because it did not restrict U.S. flexibility in structuring its forces. Democrats have also praised the treaty because it demonstrates a continuing U.S. commitment to the arms control process; many also hoped it would represent a first step on a path to deeper nuclear weapons reductions.

The Senate could, nonetheless, have amended the treaty or added conditions to its Resolution of Ratification to address perceived weaknesses.[61] The Senate Foreign Relations Committee did not recommend any amendments to the treaty. The Senate Foreign Relations Committee did, however, include reservations and conditions in the Resolution of Ratification that it approved, by a vote of 19-0, on February 5, 2003. In response to Members' concerns about the absence of timelines and interim limits in the treaty, the Resolution requires that the President report to Congress each year on the progress that the United States and Russia have made in reducing their forces to the treaty's limits. The Resolution also contains non-binding declarations that require, among other things, that the United States reduce its forces as quickly as possible and that it provide Russia with assistance in securing its non-strategic nuclear weapons would only affect U.S. policy. The full Senate approved the Resolution of Ratification, by a vote of 95-0 on March 6, 2003, with these reservations and declarations included. Some Senators proposed amendments to the Resolution of Ratification, but these were all defeated after the Chairman and Ranking Member, Senators Lugar and Biden, made it clear that they would not support any amendments to the treaty or the Resolution of Ratification during the debate on the floor of the Senate. The Text of the Resolution of Ratification appears in **Appendix B**, at the end of this report.

---

[61] For a review of the Ratification process, and the Senate's options, see U.S. Senate, Committee on Foreign Relations. *Treaties and Other International Agreements: The Role of the United States Senate.* Committee Print S. Prt. 106-71. January 2001.

The Russian Duma has also demonstrated its independence on arms control Treaties. It delayed its vote on the START II Treaty for seven years, questioning both the foreign policies of President Yeltsin and several key elements of the treaty.[62] When it did approve the treaty, it included a condition in its Federal Law on Ratification that stated Russia would not exchange the instruments of ratification, and allow the treaty to enter into force, until the United States approved several 1997 agreements related to the ABM Treaty. Since the Senate never addressed or approved these agreements, START II could not enter into force.

The Duma could have included conditions in its approval of the new treaty, as well. It did raise questions about Russia's financing and support for its strategic nuclear forces. The Duma also delayed its debate and vote on the treaty in March 2003, after the United States began its military operation in Iraq. However, most analysts agreed that neither the Duma nor the Federation Council was likely to challenge President Putin by threatening to reject the treaty. President Putin had much broader and stronger support in the Duma than President Yeltsin had. Although the leader of the Communist Party denounced the treaty as a betrayal of Russian interests, most Members who commented praised the President for convincing the United States to sign a "legally binding" treaty. In addition, Russian officials established a Working Group, which includes members of both the Duma and the Federation Council, to review the treaty and meet with government experts. This Working Group prepared the draft Federal Law on Ratification for the treaty.[63] The Duma approved the Federal Law on Ratification on May 14, 2003.

The treaty entered into force on June 1, 2003. Although it was due to remain in force until December 31, 2012, it may lapse in early 2011. In 2010, the United States and Russia signed a new START Treaty.[64] The Moscow Treaty will lapse when this new treaty enters into force. The U.S. Senate gave its consent to the ratification of the New START treaty on December 22, 2010. If the Russian parliament does the same, the New START could enter into force in early 2011.

Response and Reaction

Many analysts and observers in the United States and Russia praised the Moscow Treaty as a "useful first step" in the process of reducing U.S. and Russian nuclear weapons. They were particularly appreciative of the fact that the agreement was a formal treaty—it carried the weight of law since it was reviewed and approved by the nations' legislative bodies and it will remain in force beyond the terms of President Bush and President Putin. Some Russian commentators have also noted that, as a treaty, the document would carry more weight in the international political community, demonstrating that the United States and Russia remain committed to nuclear disarmament, as they promised in the Nuclear Nonproliferation Treaty.

Some, in both the United States and Russia, criticized the absence of provisions that would require the elimination of delivery vehicles or warheads. Some in Russia argued that this would place Russia at a disadvantage, because Russia would have to eliminate its weapons systems due to a lack of funding, but the United States will retain a "redeployment potential" with both extra

---

[62] For details, see CRS Report 97-359, *START II Debate in the Russian Duma: Issues and Prospects*, by Amy F. Woolf.

[63] On Meeting of Working Group of State Duma of the Federal Assembly on Preparation of Draft Federal Law on Ratification of the SOR Treaty, Press Release. Ministry of Foreign Affairs of the Russian Federation. January 21, 2003.

[64] For details on this treaty, see CRS Report R41219, *The New START Treaty: Central Limits and Key Provisions*, by Amy F. Woolf.

delivery capacity and extra warheads.[65] Others, in both the United States and Russia, argued that the retention of excess warheads in storage might create potential new risks because the warheads could be sold to or stolen by terrorist organizations.[66]

In Russia, some praised the treaty because it signaled the end of the START II Treaty and its ban on MIRVed ICBMs. They noted that, under the new agreement, Russia will be able to structure its forces as it sees fit. In particular, it could retain aging MIRVed ICBMs, such as the SS-18 or SS-19, or it could deploy the new SS-27 and RS-24 with multiple warheads.[67] In the United States, however, critics have argued that the demise of the ban on MIRVed ICBMs could undermine confidence and stability. They noted that multiple warhead missiles would still be an attractive target and, fearing that it might lose these weapons in an attack, Russia could still keep them at a high state of alert. This could increase the chance of an inadvertent launch of nuclear weapons in response to false or ambiguous information.[68] Furthermore, some have argued that the arms control opponents in the United States could use deployment of new MIRVed ICBMs in Russia as a reason to add warheads to the U.S. force, which could undermine the agreement and lead to its collapse.

Finally, many analysts in the United States and Russia noted that the new treaty did nothing to count, contain, or reduce non-strategic nuclear weapons—the shorter range missiles and artillery. Reports indicate that Russia may have 3,800 of these weapons and some analysts argue they are housed in storage areas that might be at risk for loss through theft or attack. Analysts also note that these weapons have played a greater role in Russia's national security policy in recent years, and that Russia might use these weapons in a conflict if it lacked the necessary conventional forces. In response to concerns about Russia's nonstrategic nuclear weapons, the Bush Administration noted that the subject would be on the agenda for discussion between the two countries.[69] The summit did not address this issue in its public documents. But Secretaries Powell and Rumsfeld both noted, during their testimony before the Senate Foreign Relations Committee, that the issue of nonstrategic nuclear weapons was likely to be high on the agenda of the new Consultative Group for Strategic Stability, which was established in the summit's Joint Declaration. Discussions on this issue, did not, however, occur.

The Road Ahead

The State Department has provided Congress with several reports on the implementation of the Strategic Offensive Reductions Treaty, as mandated by the treaty's resolution of ratification.[70]

---

[65] Golotyuk, Yuri. "By Washington's Count," *Vremya Novostey*. April 12, 2002. Translated in FBIS CEP20020412000315. See also, Sergey Rogov. "Capitulation or Move Toward Partnership? Mocow Must Use the 'Window of Opportunity.'" *Nezavisimaya Gazeta*. May 24, 2002. Translated in FBIS CEP20020524000146.

[66] Senator Joseph Biden has written "we don't want Russia to maintain excess weapons or warheads. And we do want Russia to keep the weapons it maintains out of the wrong hands." See Biden, Joseph. R. Jr. "Beyond the Moscow Treaty," *Washington Post*. May 28, 2002. p. 17. See also Odnokolenko, Oleg. Exchange of Strategic Gifts. Itogi. May 21, 2002. Translated in FBIS CEP20020521000407.

[67] Rogov, Sergey. "Capitulation or Move Toward Partnership? Mocow Must Use the 'Window of Opportunity.'" *Nezavisimaya Gazeta*. May 24, 2002. Translated in FBIS CEP20020524000146.

[68] Biden, Joseph. R. Jr. "Beyond the Moscow Treaty," *Washington Post*. May 28, 2002. p. 17.

[69] Raum, Tom. "Tactical Weapons Next Topic," *Moscow Times*. May 20, 2002. p. 5.

[70] See, for example, U.S. Department of State. Bureau of Verification, Compliance, and Implementation. 2008 Annual Report on Implementation of the Moscow Treaty. May 13, 2008. http://www.state.gov/t/vci/rls/rpt/104637 htm.

These reports indicate that both the United States and Russia were on a pace to complete their implementation well before the deadline of 2012. In a report issued in mid-2009, the State Department reported that the United States had already reduced its operationally deployed strategic nuclear warheads to a total of 2,126 warheads.[71]

During the ratification process for the Moscow Treaty, the Bush Administration assured Congress that the United States and Russia would confer frequently about the status of their nuclear forces and about their broader strategic relationship. Few of these talks occurred, however. The treaty's bilateral implementation commission rarely met, in part because the treaty contains so few rules and definitions, that compliance questions are unlikely and the parties have little to discuss as they reduce their forces. In addition, the two nations reportedly disbanded a strategic offensive transparency working group, which was slated to address monitoring and verification issues under the treaty, and instead, replaced it with a new channel of talks between Undersecretary of State Robert Joseph and John Rood and Russian Deputy Foreign Minister Sergei Kislyak. These talks also served as the forum for discussions on the future of arms control after the START Treaty expires in 2009.

The 1994 START Treaty contained a wide variety of monitoring and verification provisions that were supposed to help the nations monitor compliance with the Moscow Treaty. In the 2005 Implementation Report, the State Department noted that the START verification regime provided "important data" for the United States in its monitoring of the Moscow Treaty. The 2006 report, however, downplayed the value of the START data, indicating that the START provisions provide "additional data" that can be of use when monitoring the Moscow Treaty. This distinction is important, as some analysts have argued that the United States and Russia should at least extend the monitoring provisions in START through the 2012 end of the Moscow Treaty. Russia has gone further, calling for a new treaty that would replace START and contain many of the same types of details and definitions that were present in START but absent from the Moscow Treaty.

The Bush Administration rejected Russia's position, and instead proposed that the two sides continue implementing some of the monitoring activities to assist with the verification of compliance with the Moscow Treaty. The Obama Administration, in contrast, pursued formal negotiations with Russia, with the goal of replacing the START Treaty with a new treaty that would contain both further reductions in strategic nuclear weapons and a wide range of monitoring and verification provisions.[72] The United States and Russia signed the New START Treaty on April 8, 2010.

---

[71] U.S. State Department, Bureau of Verification and Compliance, *The Legacy of START and Related U.S. Policies*, Fact Sheet, Washington, D.C., July 16, 2009, http://www.state.gov/t/vci/rls/126119.htm.

[72] For more information on these discussions, and the issues associated with the expiration of START, see CRS Report R40084, *Strategic Arms Control After START: Issues and Options*, by Amy F. Woolf.

Appendix A. Text of Strategic Offensive Reductions Treaty

The United States of America and the Russian Federation, hereinafter referred to as the Parties,

Embarking upon the path of new relations for a new century and committed to the goal of strengthening their relationship through cooperation and friendship,

Believing that new global challenges and threats require the building of a qualitatively new foundation for strategic relations between the Parties,

Desiring to establish a genuine partnership based on the principles of mutual security, cooperation, trust, openness, and predictability,

Committed to implementing significant reductions in strategic offensive arms,

Proceeding from the Joint Statements by the President of the United States of America and the President of the Russian Federation on Strategic Issues of July 22, 2001 in Genoa and on a New Relationship between the United States and Russia of November 13, 2001 in Washington,

Mindful of their obligations under the Treaty Between the United States of America and the Union of Soviet Socialist Republics on the Reduction and Limitation of Strategic Offensive Arms of July 31, 1991, hereinafter referred to as the START Treaty,

Mindful of their obligations under Article VI of the Treaty on the Non-Proliferation of Nuclear Weapons of July 1, 1968, and

Convinced that this Treaty will help to establish more favorable conditions for actively promoting security and cooperation, and enhancing international stability,

Have agreed as follows:

Article I

Each Party shall reduce and limit strategic nuclear warheads, as stated by the President of the United States of America on November 13, 2001 and as stated by the President of the Russian Federation on November 13, 2001 and December 13, 2001 respectively, so that by December 31, 2012 the aggregate number of such warheads does not exceed 1700-2200 for each Party. Each Party shall determine for itself the composition and structure of its strategic offensive arms, based on the established aggregate limit for the number of such warheads.

Article II

The Parties agree that the START Treaty remains in force in accordance with its terms.

Article III

For purposes of implementing this Treaty, the Parties shall hold meetings at least twice a year of a Bilateral Implementation Commission.

Article IV

1. This Treaty shall be subject to ratification in accordance with the constitutional procedures of each Party. This Treaty shall enter into force on the date of the exchange of instruments of ratification.

2. This Treaty shall remain in force until December 31, 2012 and may be extended by agreement of the Parties or superseded earlier by a subsequent agreement.

3. Each Party, in exercising its national sovereignty, may withdraw from this Treaty upon three months written notice to the other Party.

Article V

This Treaty shall be registered pursuant to Article 102 of the Charter of the United Nations.

Done at Moscow on May 24, 2002, in two copies, each in the English and Russian languages, both texts being equally authentic.

Appendix B. Resolution of Ratification for the Treaty of Moscow

Resolved, (two thirds of the Senators present concurring therein),

SECTION 1. SENATE ADVICE AND CONSENT SUBJECT TO CONDITIONS AND DECLARATIONS.

The Senate advises and consents to the ratification of the Treaty Between the United States of America and the Russian Federation on Strategic Offensive Reductions (T. Doc. 107-8, in this resolution referred to as the "Moscow Treaty" or "Treaty"), subject to the conditions in section 2 and declarations in section 3.

SEC. 2. CONDITIONS.

The advice and consent of the Senate to the ratification of the Moscow Treaty is subject to the following conditions, which shall be binding on the President:

(1) REPORT ON THE ROLE OF COOPERATIVE THREAT REDUCTION AND NONPROLIFERATION ASSISTANCE. Recognizing that implementation of the Moscow Treaty is the sole responsibility of each party, not later than 60 days after the exchange of instruments of ratification of the Treaty, and annually thereafter on February 15, the President shall submit to the Committee on Foreign Relations and the Committee on Armed Services of the Senate a report and recommendations on how United States Cooperative Threat Reduction assistance to the Russian Federation can best contribute to enabling the Russian Federation to implement the Treaty efficiently and maintain the security and accurate accounting of its nuclear weapons and weapons-usable components and material in the current year. The report shall be submitted in both unclassified and, as necessary, classified form. (2) Annual implementation report. Not later than 60 days after exchange of instruments of ratification of the Treaty, and annually thereafter on April 15, the President shall submit to the Committee on Foreign Relations and the Committee on Armed Services of the Senate a report on implementation of the Treaty by the United States and the Russian Federation. This report shall be submitted in both unclassified and, as necessary, classified form and shall include

> (A) a listing of strategic nuclear weapons force levels of the United States, and a best estimate of the strategic nuclear weapons force levels of the Russian Federation, as of December 31 of the preceding calendar year;

> (B) a detailed description, to the extent possible, of strategic offensive reductions planned by each party for the current calendar year;

> (C) to the extent possible, the plans of each party for achieving by December 31, 2012, the strategic offensive reductions required by Article I of the Treaty;

> (D) measures, including any verification or transparency measures, that have been taken or have been proposed by a party to assure each party of the other party's continued intent and ability to achieve by December 31, 2012, the strategic offensive reductions required by Article I of the Treaty;

(E) information relevant to implementation of this Treaty that has been learned as a result of Strategic Arms Reduction Treaty (START) verification measures, and the status of consideration of extending the START verification regime beyond December 2009;

(F) any information, insufficiency of information, or other situation that may call into question the intent or the ability of either party to achieve by December 31, 2012, the strategic offensive reductions required by Article I of the Treaty; and

(G) any actions that have been taken or have been proposed by a party to address concerns listed pursuant to subparagraph (F) or to improve the implementation and effectiveness of the Treaty.

SEC. 3. DECLARATIONS.

The advice and consent of the Senate to the ratification of the Moscow Treaty is subject to the following declarations, which express the intent of the Senate:

(1) TREATY INTERPRETATION. The Senate reaffirms condition (8) of the resolution of ratification of the Document Agreed Among the States Parties to the Treaty on Conventional Armed Forces in Europe (CFE) of November 19, 1990 (adopted at Vienna on May 31, 1996), approved by the Senate on May 14, 1997, relating to condition (1) of the resolution of ratification of the Intermediate-Range Nuclear Forces (INF) Treaty, approved by the Senate on May 27, 1988.

(2) FURTHER STRATEGIC ARMS REDUCTIONS. The Senate encourages the President to continue strategic offensive reductions to the lowest possible levels consistent with national security requirements and alliance obligations of the United States.

(3) BILATERAL IMPLEMENTATION ISSUES. The Senate expects the executive branch of the Government to offer regular briefings, including consultations before meetings of the Bilateral Implementation Commission, to the Committee on Foreign Relations and the Committee on Armed Services of the Senate on any implementation issues related to the Moscow Treaty. Such briefings shall include a description of all efforts by the United States in bilateral forums and through diplomatic channels with the Russian Federation to resolve any such issues and shall include a description of

(A) the issues raised at the Bilateral Implementation Commission, within 30 days after such meetings;

(B) any issues related to implementation of this Treaty that the United States is pursuing in other channels, including the Consultative Group for Strategic Security established pursuant to the Joint Declaration of May 24, 2002, by the Presidents of the United States and the Russian Federation; and

(C) any Presidential determination with respect to issues described in subparagraphs (A) and (B).

(4) NONSTRATEGIC NUCLEAR WEAPONS. Recognizing the difficulty the United States has faced in ascertaining with confidence the number of nonstrategic nuclear weapons maintained by the Russian Federation and the security of those weapons, the Senate urges the President to engage the Russian Federation with the objectives of

(A) establishing cooperative measures to give each party to the Treaty improved confidence regarding the accurate accounting and security of nonstrategic nuclear weapons maintained by the other party; and

(B) providing United States or other international assistance to help the Russian Federation ensure the accurate accounting and security of its nonstrategic nuclear weapons.

(5) ACHIEVING REDUCTIONS. Recognizing the transformed relationship between the United States and the Russian Federation and the significantly decreased threat posed to the United States by the Russian Federation's strategic nuclear arsenal, the Senate encourages the President to accelerate United States strategic force reductions, to the extent feasible and consistent with United States national security requirements and alliance obligations, in order that the reductions required by Article I of the Treaty may be achieved prior to December 31, 2012.

(6) CONSULTATIONS. Given the Senate's continuing interest in this Treaty and in continuing strategic offensive reductions to the lowest possible levels consistent with national security requirements and alliance obligations of the United States, the Senate urges the President to consult with the Senate prior to taking actions relevant to paragraphs 2 or 3 of Article IV of the Treaty.

Author Contact Information

Amy F. Woolf
Specialist in Nuclear Weapons Policy
awoolf@crs.loc.gov, 7-2379